BiBLE AD

Prophets with Impact, Part I

WiTH REID THE SCROLL

by Nicki Frederiksen

BIBLE ADVENTURES WITH REID THE SCROLL, PART I
Copyright © 2019 by Nicki Frederiksen

Scripture quotations labelled NIV are taken from the Holy Bible, NEW INTERNATIONAL VERSION®, NIV® Copyright © 1973, 1978, 1984, 2011 by Biblica, Inc.® Used by permission. All rights reserved worldwide. Scripture quotations labelled NASB are taken from the New American Standard Bible®, Copyright © 1960, 1962, 1963, 1968, 1971, 1972, 1973, 1975, 1977, 1995 by The Lockman Foundation. Used by permission.

Printed in Canada

Print ISBN: 978-1-4866-1826-2
eBook ISBN: 978-1-4866-1827-9

Word Alive Press
119 De Baets Street, Winnipeg, MB R2J 3R9
www.wordalivepress.ca

Cataloguing in Publication may be obtained through Library and Archives Canada

DEDICATION

I would like to dedicate this book to my mom and dad. I am so thankful for the faith foundation they gave me. That faith has made me who I am today. My prayer is that I will pass that faith on to my son, Evan, and all the other children the Lord has placed in my life. I would like to thank my brother, who helped me create Reid the Scroll and bring him to life. Finally, I would like to thank my husband, who has supported me every step of the way throughout this writing journey.

CONTENTS

PREFACE

I have a few motivations behind writing this book. First, I want to write and deliver a message that will inspire the next generation to fall in love with God, and maybe even to write about it. I want to remind children that Jesus has written a story for them—one that they can be excited about. I want them to anticipate great things for the future.

I have had the great pleasure of becoming a "Great Auntie Nicki" to my niece's daughter. I want her to know that Jesus has a great plan for her life and that His mighty hands of protection have been over her since before she was born. This truth has sometimes become lost in a world that is fast-paced, technology-driven, and convenience-based. We sometimes lose sight of our Creator, who loves us and cares for us beyond our understanding.

Second, I desire this book to be a vehicle to connect children with their parents, grandparents, guardians, aunts, and uncles.

TO THE READER

My desire is for the creation of family memories centred on the Word of God.

Many parents are aware of the importance of reading with their children and having quality time with them. The Bible is the ultimate truth; when families read biblical stories together, learn together, and pray together, their relationships will be stronger. Part of the foundation of strong relationships is having good, healthy conversations about topics with children that not only teach them biblical principles, but also show us how to apply those principles in their lives.

My prayer is that this book will outline principles and explain how it applies to our lives. My hope is that you will learn and pray together and bless your children with a strong faith foundation in Jesus Christ.

Each chapter is divided into seven sections:

1. Principle
2. A Closer Look
3. Challenge for Children
4. Challenge for Parents or Caregiver
5. Prayer
6. A Scroll into the New Testament
7. One Step Further

You can read the book from start to finish, or you can select a chapter to read on its own and start a conversation with your children.

Instructions for Children

The most important thing you will ever hear is that you are a gift from God, and that He has great plans for you. I pray that you can read this book with your mom, dad, brother or sister, aunt, uncle, grandmother, grandfather or friend.

The Lord Jesus has an exciting journey for you to take through the Bible. The more you know about the Bible, the more you will understand your purpose—your reason for being here—and how to live a life that pleases God. God's purpose for your life is unique and special to you. Enjoy this adventure with Reid the Scroll and what God has in store for you!

For you created my inmost parts; you knit me together in my mother's womb.

—Psalm 139:13, NIV

Instructions for Parents

I believe that each of you has a great opportunity. The Bible holds the most important words your children will ever hear and learn. I pray that the Holy Spirit will bless your time together and that you will experience the Old Testament in a brand-new way.

Call to me and I will answer you and tell you great and unsearchable things you do not know.

—Jeremiah 33:3, NIV

Chapter One

NOAH: FOLLOWING INSTRUCTIONS

"Hi, boys and girls! My name is Reid the Scroll. Thanks for joining me on this adventure. The first principle I want to look at with you is following instructions. To get a better understanding of following instructions, let's look at the meaning of 'instructions.'"

Principle: The meaning of "instruction" is the directions given by a parent, teacher, adult, or instructor, and then following them. This is an important principle for the world we live in and for the plans God has for us. Let's see how following instructions works in our lives and what God has in store for you!

A Closer Look: The Story of Noah
(Genesis 6:9, 22, 7:1, 5)

Reid encourages you to open your bible to this story in the book of Genesis. Noah was a righteous man, blameless among the people of his time, and he walked with God. Noah did everything just as God commanded him, including building the ark.

"The Lord then said to Noah, 'Go into the ark, you and your whole family, because I have found you righteous in this generation" (Genesis 7:1).

Important reminder from Reid: Reid wants you to remember the importance of reading Scripture often.

Challenge for Children: As children, you will be following instructions all through your lives. God had very clear instructions for Noah. Now that you have read the story of Noah, you should know that God also has a great plan for you and special instructions for you to follow. Be the kind of person who follows the Lord's instructions. Be the kind of person who learns from those instructions and prays to follow the Lord.

Challenge for Parents or Caregiver: Read the story of Noah (Genesis 6:9, 22, 7:1, 5) in the Bible with your children. Noah was a man who had strong character and who followed instructions well (Genesis 6:9). Remind your children that Noah is a great example of an obedient man who modelled great behaviour.

God has given us prophets like Noah as examples of men and women who followed His instructions in difficult situations. Talk with your children about what happens when we don't follow instructions. "What would have happened to Noah and his family if he didn't follow instructions? If he didn't build the ark at all?" Commit the principle of instruction to prayer. Pray and ask God to help your children to follow the instructions that God has given us.

Prayer: "Dear Lord, I pray that [child's name] will follow instructions like Noah did, and that he/she will receive Your favour, just as Noah found favour in Your eyes (Genesis 6:8). Amen."

Now let's take a look at the New Testament, and what it says on following instructions!

A Scroll into the New Testament: I believe that God wants each and every one of us to go on an adventure with Him through the Old Testament and the New Testament. Look at what Jesus has to say about instructions in the New Testament: "All Scripture is God-breathed" (2 Timothy 3:16–17, NIV).

Let's take it a step further.

One Step Further: You will probably hear other kids who decide not to follow instructions from leaders, teachers, and other people in charge. Rules are there to keep us and others safe and to help us make good decisions. Be a rule-follower and ask God to help you help other kids follow the rules, too.

Chapter Two

ABRAHAM: TRUSTING GOD'S PLANS

> "I hope you had fun learning about the principle of following instructions. Now it's time to look at the principle of trusting God's plans!"
>
> Remember, God's ways are the best ways and He has your best interest in mind.

Principle: To "trust" means to rely on someone or something without having any doubt or concerns, and believing them. God is *omnipotent*—that means that He has unlimited power and is able to do anything! God can be trusted, and His plans for you are better than you could even imagine. God has His hand on your life.

The meaning of "direction" or "plan" is an outline of what you need to do to accomplish your goal or plan by someone. The "someone" is God, and you can trust in His management and His plans. He is the ultimate guide.

A Closer Look: The Story of Abraham
(Genesis 12:1)

Reid encourages you to open your bible to this story in the book of Genesis. In Genesis 12, the Lord said to Abram:

"Go from your country, your people and your father's household to the land I will show you. 'I will make you a great nation, and I will bless you; I will make your name great, and you will be a blessing. I will bless those who bless you, and whoever curses you I will curse; and all the peoples on earth will be blessed through you.'"

—Genesis 12:1–3, NIV

Important Reminder from Reid: Reid says, the more you read Scripture, the more it will be rooted in your heart.

Challenge for Children: Abraham was called by God to do something very important. In the story of Abraham, we learned about what God told him to do, and how he would be blessed in his obedience (which means to obey). Each of you is called by God to do something special and unique. You are called to pray, serve, put others first, love your enemies, do the right thing, be thankful, be responsible, do your best in school, help around the house, be kind to others, and many other things. God also wants to bless you in amazing and wonderful ways.

Challenge for Parents or Caregiver: Read the story of Abraham in the Bible with your children (Genesis 12:1). It is so important to speak to our children about listening to God's voice, and to His callings in our lives and our children's lives.

We are living in a world where kids are being pulled in every direction, and those directions aren't always ideal. We need to be talking to our children about hearing God's voice and His direction. Encourage your children to talk about what God is saying to them and to make the decision to follow what God says.

Commit the principle of trusting God's plans to prayer. Pray and ask God to help your children follow this principle.

Prayer: "I pray that [child's name] will follow the Lord's leading every day of his/her life, just like Abraham did as he went to a far-off land (Genesis 12:1). I pray that [child's name] will be a blessing to others, just as You said that Abraham would be a blessing to the world. Amen."

Now let's take a look at what the New Testament has to say about this principle!

A Scroll into the New Testament: The Bible says we are called to be imitators of the Lord. This means that we need to act like Him. Think about how you can make a difference in the world around you by being like Jesus and showing His love to others. *"Be imitators of me, just as I also am of Christ"* (1 Corinthians 11:1, NASB).

Let's take it a step further.

One Step Further: Each of us has our own plans. We like to do things our way. There will be times when we have to make decisions to take a different path from our friends. It might not be to a different land, like it was for Abraham, but it could be listening to God and asking God to help you with a tough situation.

Praying is the best place to start. Then, take a step of courage and see what God will do!

Chapter Three

JOSEPH: FORGIVENESS

> "There is so much to learn, and I love to learn with you! The next principle is an important one—and might be a difficult one."

Principle: This principle is forgiveness. If you decide to follow it, this principle can take a bad situation and turn it to something good. Let's learn more about this principle!

Forgiveness happens when you choose to stop feeling angry or resentful towards someone for something they did to hurt you, intentionally or unintentionally. Let's take a closer look at forgiveness through the story of Joseph.

A Closer Look: The Story of Joseph
(Genesis 37:1–5, 12, 50:19)

Reid encourages you to open your bible to this story in the book of Genesis. There was a man named Joseph. Joseph's father, Israel, loved Joseph more than he loved his other sons. Joseph's brothers knew how much their father loved him, and they would not speak a kind word about him because of their jealousy.

Joseph told his brothers about the dreams he had about being the favourite and the brothers hated him even more. They sold him into slavery because of their hatred. Later, we read that while Joseph was in prison, the Lord was still with him; God showed him kindness and granted him favour.

Important Reminder from Reid: The more you read the Bible, the more you will understand God's plan for your life.

Challenge for Children: Our world will be a better place when you learn to be a forgiving person. Joseph dealt with a very difficult situation, as we read in his story. Joseph could have handled his brothers' hatred very differently, but it was only by the grace of God that Joseph forgave them (Genesis 50:19).

People in your life will hurt your feelings and make you mad or sad. But being someone who forgives will help you have healthier and stronger relationships, and help your friends see Jesus in you.

Challenge for Parents or Caregiver: Read the story of Joseph in the Bible with your children (Genesis 50:19). Our children are watching us all the time—what we do and how we behave. Be an example of someone who gives and receives forgiveness. Extend grace and mercy to others, just like Joseph did to his brothers (Genesis 50:19).

When your children can see you forgiving and when they can receive forgiveness, it will change their lives. Commit the principle of forgiveness to prayer. Ask God to help your kids follow the principle of forgiveness.

Prayer: "Dear Lord, please help me as a parent to model forgiveness to [child's name]. I pray that he/she will be a person like Joseph, who extends forgiveness often and with sincerity. Amen."

Now let's take a look at what the New Testament has to say about this principle!

A Scroll into the New Testament: God commands us to forgive others, just as He forgave us. No one is perfect—people will let you down or hurt your feelings. But if you can forgive instead of hate, God's love will shine through you. *"For if you forgive other people when they sin against you, your heavenly Father will also forgive you"* (Matthew 6:14, NIV).

Let's take it a step further.

One Step Further: It is one thing to forgive a person, but it is a very different thing to forgive *and* forget. Ask the Lord to help you forgive and forget. Only God can change the way you think and the way you act. He will help you to leave the past behind.

Chapter Four

MOSES: GOD'S PROTECTION

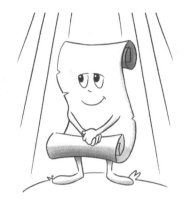

"I love to learn with you, boys and girls! It is so important that we pay close attention to these different biblical principles. I hope this principle will give you a better understanding of God's protection over your life."

Principle: God is always protecting you, which means keeping you safe. God's protection is unique and different because He created us, and no one in the world can protect us like He does. It is helpful to think about how our parents protect us. In most situations, parents will do everything they can to keep their children safe. God has a way of protecting us that is hard to understand, but He also protects us in a way that only He can. Let's read about how God promised to protect Moses!

A Closer Look: The Story of Moses
(Exodus 1:22, 2:1–3)

Reid encourages you to open your bible to this story in the book of Exodus. There was a man and a woman from the tribe of Levi who got married. The woman became pregnant and had a son, and she named him Moses. She saw that he was a fine child.

At this time, Pharaoh commanded that all baby boys be put to death, so the woman had to hide her baby for three months. Moses's mom placed him in the Nile River, believing that God would protect him—and He did! God worked it out so that not only would Moses grow up in the palace, but His own mother could look after him while he was young.

> Important reminder from Reid: We are changed as we read Scripture, and God is turning us into the person/creation He wants us to be.

Challenge for Children: God protects us every day of our lives. Sometimes this is hard to understand, because we don't *see* God. But He does love us, and He protects us every moment of every day. As we read, God protected Moses in a very special way during a very scary time for his family. God, the Creator of the entire universe, is protecting you all the time.

Challenge for Parents or Caregiver: Read the story of Moses in the Bible with your children (Exodus 1:22, 2:1–3). As parents, we need to regularly tell our children that God is with them and that He will never leave them. I believe that when  this foundational truth is spoken into our children's lives on a regular basis, it will change the way they think and the way they live their lives.

Many children these days experience anxiety, which is difficult for a child to handle. When our children know that God, their

Creator, is watching over them, they will feel comfort and peace, not fear or anxiety. It will transform them, allowing the Holy Spirit to work in their lives.

Commit the principle of protection to prayer. Pray and ask God to help you understand how to receive His promise of protection.

Prayer: "Dear Lord, I pray that [child's name] will remember that God's hand of protection is always over his/her life. You went to great lengths to protect Moses, and You do the same for us, too. Thank You for all the ways You protect us every day. Amen."

Now let's take a look at the New Testament and what it teaches about God's protection!

A Scroll into the New Testament: The Bible says that the Lord will strengthen us and protect us. We need to receive this truth and not allow fear to get in the way of God's plans for us. *"But the Lord is faithful, and he will strengthen you and protect you from the evil one"* (2 Thessalonians 3:3, NIV).

Let's take it a step further.

One Step Further: Make a point every day to thank God for His mighty protection over your life. God has an amazing way of protecting us every day. Reminding ourselves of this truth daily will help us to remember that He will never leave us when we need Him.

Chapter Five

JOSHUA: FOLLOWING THE DIRECTIONS OF YOUR LEADERS

"Thanks for joining me again! This principle has a personal touch to it, as it is all about the people God places in your life to help you succeed. Let's take a closer look at following directions!"

Principle: When a parent or other adult shows you the way you should go, whether at home, at school, or at other activities, this is giving direction. God will put people in your life to guide and direct you throughout your life. It is part of the exciting journey God has in mind for you.

Now let's take a look at how Joshua followed the directions of his leaders.

A Closer Look: The Story of Joshua
(Genesis 34:9)

 Reid encourages you to open your bible to this story in the book of Genesis. Moses invested in Joshua's life. (To "invest" means to spend time and energy to make something or someone better.) This investment was preparing Joshua to serve God. God's plan for Joshua was to fill him with hope and a future (Jeremiah 29:11), preparing him for the different parts in his journey.

Little did Joshua know what was ahead for him, as God used Moses to lead and direct him. It is pretty incredible to think that because of Moses's investment in Joshua, the Israelites listened to Joshua and did has he commanded (Genesis 34:9).

The leaders in *your* life will have great impact on your life journey and how God wants to use you for His glory.

 **Challenge for Children:** The Lord puts leaders— or people we can trust—in our lives for a reason. Joshua was chosen to lead the people of Israel, but he learned from and trusted the advice of Moses. Moses was Joshua's mentor.

These kinds of relationships are very important, and God will teach you different things through the leaders in your life. These leaders at church will teach you about God's truth. At school, it could be a teacher who confirms a skill that you are good at. Pay close attention to how God is using leaders in your life—just like Joshua listened to and followed the direction of Moses.

Important reminder from Reid: Reid wants to encourage you by reminding you that God has great plans for you and your life. The Bible is His gift to you for your life journey.

Challenge for Parents or Caregiver: Read the story of Joshua in the Bible with your children (Genesis 34:9). Leaders in your children's lives have been handpicked by the Lord. Encourage your children with this truth and let them know that they can trust what they learn from those leaders, *as long as it lines up with what God says in the Bible.*

The Lord has placed these mentors in their lives for a reason, and we need to encourage and nurture those relationships. Commit the principle of following instructions and respecting the authority of leaders to prayer. Pray and ask God to help your child understand this principle.

 **Prayer:** "Dear Father, I pray that [child's name] will be aware of the leaders who have been placed in his/her life and will listen to their direction. Help him/her to learn from these mentors and to grow in wisdom. Thank You for the mentors You will place in [child's name]'s life and help him/her to have a teachable spirit. Amen."

Now let's take a look at the New Testament to learn more about this principle!

A Scroll into the New Testament: At different times in your children's lives, they will have a variety of leaders. Regularly talk to your children about these people, the impact they are having, and how that affects their lives. *"Obey your leaders and submit to them, for they keep watch over you and your souls"* (Hebrews 13:17, NASB).

Let's take it a step further.

One Step Further: Our children need to learn how to connect or engage with the leaders in their lives. This can start with regularly telling your children to thank their leaders for their involvement in their lives.

Remind your children that God is the One who has placed these leaders in their lives, and that this is a personal gift from Him. Talk about these relationships and ask God to bless them.

Chapter Six

GIDEON: KNOWING GOD'S WAY IS THE BEST WAY

> "There are so many ways that you can get direction in life—your family, friends, teachers, or social media. Let's look at how God's way is the best way."

Principle: Only Jesus Christ can give you the right directions. There are many different ways we can choose to go to reach a destination. There is the world's way, and there is God's way.

The Lord Jesus has a great course planned for your life. He knows you inside and out (Psalm 139) and the way you should go. Now, let's take a look at the story of Gideon, and how he learned about how God's way was the best way.

A Closer Look: The Story of Gideon
(Judges 6:12; 8:23)

Reid encourages you to open your bible to this story in the book of Judges. A highlight from the story of Gideon is when the angel of the Lord appeared to him. He was told he was a mighty warrior and that the Lord was with him. What an amazing truth to hear from God! This could have made Gideon very proud and think he was better than other people.

Instead, I believe what happened was that Gideon had respect for the Lord. No matter how strong and mighty Gideon was, these qualities could never replace the strength, power, and direction that God would give him throughout his life.

"But Gideon told them: 'I will not rule over you, nor will my son rule over you. The Lord will rule over you'" (Judges 8:23, NIV).

Important reminder from Reid: Think back to the last chapter about Joshua and how God places people in your life to give you direction. We often need help with direction. Your life journey has already started. Just like if you don't have GPS on a long journey (or any journey), without that guidance and direction, you might get lost.

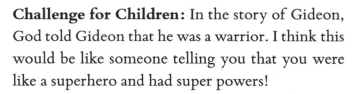

Challenge for Children: In the story of Gideon, God told Gideon that he was a warrior. I think this would be like someone telling you that you were like a superhero and had super powers!

It would probably be very easy for a person to love being a superhero and having super powers. I think it would be even easier to start thinking you could do some pretty amazing things and that you could do things your own way and not even need God.

But even with an amazing compliment from God, Gideon declared to the people of Israel that even though he was a mighty warrior, God's ways are still the *best* ways. God needs to be the ultimate authority over everyone else, and only He can give you the direction you need!

Challenge for Parents or Caregiver: Read the story of Gideon in the Bible with your children (Judges 6:12; 8:23). Be models for your children and talk regularly about how you look to the Lord for direction and guidance over the important things in your life, such as major family decisions, finances, work, and friends. As you lead by example, they will follow you.

It is time to commit the principle of direction to prayer. We are going to pray and ask God to help you follow His ways.

Prayer: "Dear Lord, I pray that [child's name] will remember that the only One who can give true direction over his/her life is You, Jesus. Help us always to remember that Your ways are higher than ours, and to follow the path You have set before us (Judges 8:23). Amen."

Now let's look at the New Testament to explore this theme further!

A Scroll into the New Testament: Choosing the right direction requires wisdom—which means making a point of connecting with the Lord daily. One of the greatest gifts that the Lord gives us is His wisdom and a direct line of communication to talk to Him—through prayer.

What an amazing opportunity to pray and ask Jesus for wisdom. He is waiting for you to ask, so don't be afraid to ask God for wisdom, and make sure you're ready to listen.

"But if any of you lacks wisdom, let him ask God" (James 1:5, NASB).

Let's take it a step further.

One Step Further: For most of us, in order to make things a habit, we need to do it many times.

Gideon told the Israelites not to look to *him* to be their ruler, but to look to *God*. The Lord is the only One who will give you the direction you need. As you spend more time in Scripture and pray, God will build good habits that will point you to Him. Let's ask God to be our leader, and then take action and follow Him.

Chapter Seven

SAMSON: LEARNING YOUR UNIQUE GIFTS

"We're learning so much together! This story is going to tell you about how unique and wonderful you are in God's eyes."

Principle: God has made each and every one of us unique; this means that each of us has something special to offer the world. These unique gifts should be used for His purpose and to glorify Him. Let's dig deeper in the story of Samson!

A Closer Look: The Story of Samson (Judges 13:5)

Reid encourages you to open your bible to this story in the book of Judges. In Judges, it says that Samson was a Nazarite, and that he was set apart by God from the day he was born. Samson was given the gift of incredible strength, but he was not supposed to cut his hair, or he would lose his gift.

Figure out what your special skill or ability might be. Talk to your parents about it, and about how you can honour God with it. Don't let anyone trick you into thinking that you don't have something special to offer. And don't let anyone tell you that your gifts are not important!

> Important reminder from Reid: Reid wants you to remind that God has a great plan for you and that the Bible is the way to figure out that plan.

Challenge for Children: Each one of you has unique gifts and abilities. You were set apart by God from the moment you were born. There are no exceptions to this—God has given each person something special to offer this world.

In the book of Judges, we read about Samson, who was set apart for God. God expected Samson to make smart decisions in order to protect his gift, and He expects you to do the same thing.

Challenge for Parents or Caregiver: We live in a world where the unique qualities of our children can be overshadowed by criticism and negative feedback. We need to encourage our children that they are unique and special in the eyes of the Lord and that they are the apple of His eye (Psalm 17:8).

Use your God-given gifts for His glory, and when you see your children using their gifts, encourage them in this behaviour. God decided to provide Samson with strength with his hair. (Judges 13:5). What are *your* children's special abilities?

Commit the principle of our unique purpose to prayer. Pray and ask God to help you understand your unique purpose.

Prayer: "Dear Lord, I pray that [child's name] will remember that he/she has gifts, skills, and abilities that You have given to use for Your glory. Help [child's name] to foster those gifts and not to be afraid to use them. Amen."

Now let's take a look at the New Testament to learn more about our unique gifts!

A Scroll into the New Testament: We all have skills and abilities. Your abilities are unique to you, and God needs you to use them by the power of the Holy Spirit. It is amazing how God will use your skills throughout your day! Watch and see what God will do.

"There are different kinds of gifts, but the same Spirit distributes them" (1 Corinthians 12:4, NIV).

Let's take it a step further.

One Step Further: It's important to figure out what your special gift is and to use it. Ask God to show you how to use these gifts. It might be a musical gift, a helping gift, or the gift of encouragement. Whatever it might be, pray and ask God about how He wants you to use it.

Some people might tell you that your gift isn't great or even worth using. Don't let other kids or adults make decisions about your

God-given talents. Remember, we won't have the same talents or gifts as other people, and that's okay—we are all unique. God created you on purpose, for a purpose!

Chapter Eight

DAVID: KNOWING WE ARE GOD'S CHOSEN ONES

"Hi, kids! I hope you're enjoying our time together. This story will help you understand that before you were born, God had something special in mind for you to do. You were chosen to do something that only *you* can do. Let's take a look at this principle together."

Principle: We are all chosen by God to do His work. Being "chosen" means having been selected to do something designed for you to do. Sometimes, the Bible uses "anointed," which means being selected by God to do something special. We are all children of God, chosen to do something special and unique. Now, let's take a look at this principle in the story of David.

A Closer Look: The Story of David
(1 Samuel 16:1–13)

Reid encourages you to open your bible to this story in the book of 1 Samuel. Samuel was given instructions to find the one chosen by God to be the next King of Israel from the family of a man named Jesse. It took some time to find David, but

Samuel still found him. David was not the most handsome or the tallest (1 Samuel 16:7), but he had a good heart—and that is what God was looking for.

> Important reminder from Reid: Reid has also learned that your parents are such an important part of your journey. Ask them questions and pray together in order to get direction from God.

Challenge for Children: God has anointed you and placed His hand of blessing on you! He's set you apart for great things.

In 1 Samuel 16, God tells the prophet Samuel to search for and find the one God has chosen to be King of Israel. Samuel went to a man named Jesse and he wanted to see his sons. Everyone thought Jesse's oldest son, Eliab, would be chosen to be the king because of how he looked: tall, strong, and handsome.

But 1 Samuel 16:7 says that people look at how someone looks on the outside, but that God looks at what is inside—the heart. God loves you and has a great plan for you. Once you invite the Lord into your heart, you have His blessing and the Holy Spirit will guide and direct you. He will do a great work in us when we let Him.

Challenge for Parents or Caregiver: As we raise our children, we need to impress upon them that they are children of the Most High God, that He loves them with an everlasting love, and that His blessing is on their lives. This is a truth that can't be changed.

God has a great plan for our children's lives and His blessing is over what they do— whether at home, at school, or in activities.

Commit the principle of being chosen to do God's work to prayer. Pray and ask God to help you understand what He has chosen you to do for Him.

Prayer: "Dear God, I pray that [child's name] remembers that Your hand is on his/her life, just like You were pleased with David and blessed him. Please show Your plan to [child's name]. Thank You, Lord, that Your life plan for him/her is amazing! (I Samuel 16:12)

Now let's take a deeper look in the New Testament!

A Scroll into the New Testament: Being anointed or blessed by Jesus will take you on an amazing adventure. Are you ready for the adventure of a lifetime? 1 John 2:27 says, *"… the anointing which you received from Him abides in you, and you have no need for anyone else to teach you"* (NASB).

Let's take it a step further.

One Step Further: People will always have an opinion about you—how you look, how you dress, what you do, how you act. Remind yourself every day that God has chosen you and that

He looks at the *inside* of a person. The Holy Spirit will work through you when you pray and call on Jesus' name.

Chapter Nine

SOLOMON: WISDOM AND MAKING WISE DECISIONS

"Are you having as much fun as I am learning about what God wants for us? Making wise decisions is part of everyday life and will lead you down a path that will honour God. Let's take a closer look at the meaning of wisdom and how God will ultimately direct you."

Principle: Wisdom is the knowledge of what is true and right, while using the right judgment. This principle can be challenging, because there are many ideas about what is right and wrong. Social media can show children different ways to handle different situations. Some children have a hard time making good judgments because they are simply unclear about what that means.

Now let's take a look at the story of Solomon and the wisdom that he had.

A Closer Look: The Story of Solomon
(1 Kings 3:5–9)

Reid encourages you to open your bible to this story in the book of 1 Kings. In 1 Kings 3 (at Gibeon), the Lord appeared to Solomon during the night in a dream, and God told him to ask for whatever he wanted God to give him. *"Solomon answered, 'You have shown me great kindness to your servant'"* (1 Kings 3:6-7, NIV).

In this conversation with God, Solomon mentions that God was faithful to his father. Later on, Solomon acknowledges that he has been given the honour of leading the Israelites. He also says he is only a child, and Solomon needed wisdom to lead the people.

> Important reminder from Reid: Reid wants you to remember to connect with your parents. Pray with them and ask for wisdom and direction in your journey.

Challenge for Children: Making good decisions is a part of everyday life. There are simple decisions, like what you are going to wear to school, and tougher decisions, like whether to forgive that friend who hurt your feelings.

Solomon's desire was to always make good decisions and to make these decisions with a spirit of humility (*not* thinking you're better than others). When you do your best to make good decisions knowing that God will direct you, the outcome of situations will likely be more positive.

Challenge for Parents or Caregiver: Children need to learn to make good decisions. We need to give them the freedom to start making their own decisions at a certain age. Most importantly, we need to help our children understand that the

Holy Spirit will guide and direct them when we ask God for help.

The sooner our children have this truth rooted in their hearts, the more likely it is that they will make decisions that are pleasing and honouring to God.

Commit the principle of making wise decisions to prayer. Pray and ask God to help you make wise decisions every day.

Prayer: "Dear God, I pray that [child's name] remembers that true wisdom comes from You. Please help [child's name] commit all situations to prayer, just like Solomon did, and guide him/her so that he/she makes wise decisions. Amen."

Now let's take a look at the New Testament
for more about wisdom!

A Scroll into the New Testament: The Lord is very clear that whoever wants wisdom needs to ask Him for it. Don't be afraid to ask—in fact, He looks forward to your prayer.

"If any of you lack wisdom, you should ask God, who gives generously to all without finding fault, and it will be given to you" (James 1:5, NIV).

Let's take it a step further.

One Step Further: We live in a world where making wise decisions can be difficult, and they might not be the most popular. Make a point of praying and asking God for direction with kids and as a family. Follow the lead of Solomon and ask the Lord for a spirit of wisdom and humility.

Chapter Ten

NEHEMIAH: BEING PART OF THE SOLUTION

"This is the last part of our journey together through the Old Testament. The story of Nehemiah can be extremely valuable to a young person who is trying to live a life that is pleasing and honouring to God. Each generation faces situations that involve problem solving at a different level."

Principle: Finding a solution means trying to find the best possible answer or outcome. This can mean trying to figure out the best way to handle something involving your brother or sister, parents, friends. Nehemiah is a great story to review and find out how he was able to find a solution.

Now let's examine the story of Nehemiah and see how our principle fits into his story!

A Closer Look: The Story of Nehemiah
(Nehemiah 2:1–6)

 Reid encourages you to open your bible to this story in the book of Nehemiah. King Artaxerxes was enjoying a meal when he noticed that Nehemiah looked troubled. Nehemiah had heard terrible things about Jerusalem—the city had been destroyed and he wanted to help.

The king asked Nehemiah if something was wrong. Verse 4 says Nehemiah first prayed to God and then answered the king, asking if he could rebuild Jerusalem's walls. The king granted his request.

> Important reminder from Reid: Reid wants you to play an active role in being part of the solution for your life journey and God's plan for you.

 **Challenge for Children:** We face problems every day. Will you be part of the problem or the solution?

We are all going to come across situations in our lives where we can help God. Nehemiah was in a very interesting situation. He had an important job as the cupbearer for the king. He heard that there were some problems in Jerusalem, and he decided to take action—to help rebuild the city and tell people to return to God.

Do you take action when you see trouble? If you see trouble with a friend, are you going to be part of the problem, or part of the solution? If there are challenges or issues at home, do you do your best to figure out a solution?

Challenge for Parents or Caregiver: Nehemiah saw a problem and found a solution. Teach your children to be aware of what is happening around them and to listen to the voice of God. When our children are trained to become problem solvers and use those techniques with prayer, they'll see super-  natural results. Commit the principle of being part of the solution to prayer. Pray and ask God to help you understand this principle.

Prayer: "Dear Lord, I pray that [child's name] will be part of Your solution. Help him/her to listen to the Holy Spirit and follow Your directions. Amen."

Now let's take a look at the New Testament for more about being a part of the solution!

A Scroll into the New Testament: Being a part of a solution is important and honours God. There are many different situations that can come up that need a solution. Your friends could be in a conflict and you can be part of the solution by telling them to value the friendship over the conflict.

You might see kids bullying other kids. You could ignore this or try to help. Telling an adult is a good place to start.

You could be involved in a school project and the kids in your group are just not getting along. Take a moment to pray and ask God to help you. Even asking a simple question to someone in the group, like, "What part are you interested in doing for this project?" could be the help that is needed to get the group working towards a solution.

The Bible talks about prayer and giving our situations to God. *"Be anxious for nothing, but in everything by prayer and supplication with thanksgiving let your requests be made known to God"* (Philippians 4:6, NASB).

One Step Further: Nehemiah was a man of prayer, especially during a time when he had to take action and determine a solution. He needed divine direction. You can also be someone who takes action through prayer. Remember the importance of prayer and be part of God's solution.

It has been so much fun journeying through the Old Testament stories with you, boys and girls! I hope this journey has allowed you to see how much God has to say to us through His Word!

Keep reading your Bible to hear what God has to say, and then pray that God can use you and let what He's teaching you to become habits! You were made for a purpose, so don't be afraid to step out boldly into everything He's calling you to do!

Until next time,
Reid the Scroll

ABOUT THE AUTHOR

Children's author Nicki Frederiksen desires to have families explore the life principles found in the Old Testament through her character, Reid the Scroll, to inspire the next generation to get excited and make a connection with these principles.

Over the past ten years, through her work in children's ministry and community programming, Nicki has honed her God-given passion and desire to tell the exciting and valuable stories and life principles found in the Old Testament, inviting families to reconnect with God's Word and strengthen their relationships with each other. She hopes to inspire children and their parents to read these biblical stories together and see how they relate directly and strategically to their lives. Join Reid the Scroll as he takes you and your family on a biblical adventure so you can impact the world, one principle at a time.

Nicki Frederiksen lives in London, Ontario, with her husband of over twenty years and their twelve-year-old son, Evan.